D1592702

Very Nice Things People are Saying about James Finn Garner:

Politically Correct Pinocchio

THE WOKE WOODEN WONDER OF OUR TIMES

POLITICALLY CORRECT PINOCCHIO

by James Finn Garner

Book design by Airan Wright
airanwright.com

Cover art by Liam Anne Garner

ISBN 978-1-7326589-0-5

To truth tellers everywhere.

And to Lies again, happily ever after.

CONTENTS

INTRODUCTION

The Golem of Prague.
Frankenstein's monster.
Mecha-Godzilla.
Pinocchio.

Bracing, cautionary tales of the chaos and destruction that can result when Man (and by that, of course, I mean men) tries to play God.

Hyperbolic? Perhaps. But, as a wise persun once said, hyperbole in the defense of hysteria is no vice. Pinocchio, the puppet who came to life, is the rosy-cheeked embodiment of our perverse desire to control and harness Nature for our own selfish ends. The only real difference between Gepetto's workshop and Dr. Frankenstein's lab is electricity and differently spinal slave labor.

(If the men in these stories wanted to create life, they might've been better off to leave their man-cave workspaces long enough to meet a living, breathing wommon for a change. Not that she should give such narcissistic, monomaniacal dweebs any attention or affection, but at least we might endure less terror among the peasant population.)

In my earlier story collections, I tried to instill in our pre-adults modes of thinking that were constructive, unbiased and wholesome. But the time for thinking has passed. With this new tale of the wooden individual animated against his will and hurled into a depraved world, I hope to spur all of us into action. We will not get (sorry for this ethnic insensitivity) a Mulligan for our lives here. This is the only earth we have on this planet, and we'd better stop relying on our big-brained "wisdom" to solve all our problems. No blue fairy will come along and make us more hummon persuns, and the only magick that I know of is the magick of storytelling.

My hope is that, by truly looking at the real messages of the stories we tell our children and ourselves, and cleansing them of the influences of the cruel, exploitative past, we will be able eventually to tell the difference between the puppets (us) and the puppet masters (probably us as well).

CHAPTER 1

*In which the hero of our story
has a shocking awakening.*

Many years ago (or not so many, because a story's worth doesn't depend on age, and many long-ignored narratives are now being told), in a picturesque little village lived a carpenter named Geppetto. His small-footprint house/workspace was neat and clean and energy efficient, in a style that would become trendy a few years later, at least among magazine art directors. Throughout his life, Geppetto had been single. He had never "taken" a wife, a lover, a mistress, a significant other or a regular sexual surrogate of any kind. When asked, Geppetto used to tell people, "I'm alone, but not lonely," and lived as a fulfilled single persun, dividing his leisure hours between positive journaling and goat yoga.

As time and experiences accumulated, however, Geppetto felt the need to pass his knowledge on to someone else, in a mentoring relationship of sorts. Since the official agencies frowned upon on an economically marginalized, 75-year-old hermit adopting a child, Geppetto decided to meet his need for company his own way. Using his two calloused and expert hands, he created an indigenous artisanal companion of his own.

He chose a log of seasoned ash, for he never used tropical hardwoods in his shop (in fact, he only carved local trees that had fallen under natural circumstances, then used recycled materials for whatever else he needed). Whistling a cheery folk tune about a labor riot, he picked up his sharp tools and began to chisel away. By the end of the evening, in a wonderful display of primitive craftspersunship, Geppetto had finished his youthful wooden chum.

"That's a good day's work," Geppetto said in a healthy, self-fulfilled way. "Tomorrow I will teach him all I know about carpentry, life, love and how to be your own best friend. And I will call him Pinocchio." He then lit a candle, turned down the thermostat, and toddled off to bed.

Just as Geppetto's head hit his ergonomically designed pillow, a quivering light appeared in his workshop and fluttered slowly in the air. From that mystickal light emerged a young wommon, bedecked in a flowing blue gown that glittered like an unpolluted sea at midday. Flicking the delicate wings that sprouted from her back, she glided over to the workbench where the puppet sat. She touched him with her powerful wand, subverting its sad, phallic imagery for her own vivifying purposes. Slowly at first, then more quickly, the puppet stirred and moved his head and blinked his eyes in wonder at everything around him.

"Hello," said the blue wommon to the persun of log.

"Wh-where am I?" the puppet asked. "Wh-who are you? Wow, are you a fairy?"

She sighed and answered, "I am an *individual* who just happens to *be* a fairy. I have many more interests and facets to my persunality than can be adequately described by some limiting label. Don't pigeonhole me with your conception of what a fairy should and should not be."

"G-gosh, I'm real sorry," he said, properly contrite.

"And don't even *think* of asking me to smile more."

"Oh, never, never!" What a world of accelerated unusualness he was now in!

The magickal wommon's demeanor softened a bit. "This is a very lucky day for you, Pinocchio."

"Hey, hold on a minute," he said. "Why do you call me that?"

"Because that is your name," she said.

"But no one consulted *me*," he protested. "That's not fair. Don't I and I alone reserve the right to name myself?"

"Of course you do," agreed the aethereal visitor. "I apologize. What name can you think of that fully describes your position in the world and your philosophy of life, and is free of the barbaric exploitation and bigoted assumptions of the inherited cultural paradigm?"

"Um . . . what?"

She fluttered a few seconds. "Just relax, and a name will come to you."

The puppet frowned in thought a minute, then declared, "I think I choose to call myself . . . Rumpelstiltskin!"

Her smile faltered. "It's been done."

"Howdy Doody?"

"Errrr . . ."

"Well," said the eager little puppet, "how about . . . Pinocchio?"

"A wise and responsible choice for a puppet of such tender years," said the reality-queer persun. "I'm glad we solved that. As I was saying, this is a very lucky day for you. You have been granted life! And if you live a correct and progressive one, avoid refined sugar and red meat, and work hard to become fully self-actualized (though definitely not at the expense of others), you will turn into a real boy!"

All this was too much for Pinocchio to grasp. So many possibilities, so many conditions, so many strings attached! Finally he said, "Wait a second. You're assuming that becoming a hummon is the be-all and end-all of

3

everything. If I were to go hominid, I'd be turning my back on my puppetal origins! I'm not sure that's what I want at all."

"You are right," apologized the wommon. "I imposed my own anthropocentric biases onto you. Life is long, Pinocchio, and you will go through many changes. When the time finally . . . "

"And what's with the gender bias? I was made with male parts — so what? Everyone knows there's a huge difference between a physical body and gender identity. Society's toxic messages of masculinity won't . . ."

"Listen! You're not my only appointment tonight. This is a side gig. When the time is right, I will appear to you again, and we can discuss your metamorphosal options at that time. Until then, consider all viewpoints, practice self-care, and stay hydrated. There is much to learn, and just as much (if not more) to unlearn. As we sometimes say around the entrepreneurial roundtable at the fairy ring, 'Now that you been woke, you gotta stay woke.'"

With that, she disappeared just as she had arrived and left Pinocchio alone to contemplate his new opportunities.

CHAPTER 2

*In which Pinocchio feels stifled by the
demands of the patriarchy and gravitates
toward the performing arts.*

The next morning, Geppetto awoke to find
that his nondenominational prayers had been
answered. The puppet he had crafted was now
alive! The wood carver picked up his new pal,
and they danced around and around for joy. When finally
they were exhausted, Geppetto explained to the wooden
individual that it was time for him to go to school and be
properly socialized.

Pinocchio, of course, objected. He protested that it was a
mistake to fill his head with outmoded ideas; that his own
intuitive reasoning would be smothered; and that all he
would learn in school would be survivor-biased propaganda,
the conformist pressures of mob thinking, and the self-
serving deceptions of dead white men. But Geppetto would
have none of it. He put a few coins in Pinocchio's hand and
sent him off to school.

On the street, Pinocchio muttered to himself about the
injustice of it all: "Why should I have to go to school just
because I happen to be alive? I didn't ask to be animated. It's
just not fair."

As he turned a corner, he came face to face with two strangers, a Fox and a Cat.

"Whatever is the matter, my dear puppet?" asked the Fox.

"My father is making me go to school against my will," was the answer. "Almost threatened me with a shellacking."

"Child abuse!" gasped the Cat.

"Who needs to go to school," the Fox said, "especially in the prime of youth?"

"Not me," said Pinocchio. "It will impede my individuality and warp my persunal expression."

"Persunal expression," agreed the Cat.

"Aha! I knew it," the Fox said in a syrupy voice. "If persunal expression is your paramount consideration, my friend, take my advice: Your sole destination should and must be . . . the theater!"

"Really?" asked Pinocchio.

"Oh, yes," the Fox intoned. "I've known and helped a number of young thespians in my day. You have such marvelous potential — you could reach millions with your gifts. Your star quality shines forth like a beacon, though your instrument is still quite green."

"A green instrument," agreed the Cat.

"Sounds pretty narcissistic to me," the puppet sneered.

"Not at all! Your story needs to be told. You should come with us to meet someone who will know exactly how to nourish your ingrained skills, a keen observer of the hummon condition, a facilitator you can trust completely."

And so they walked along, discussing the thrills of live performance, the social imperative of nontraditional casting, and whether improv had become some kind of misogynist cult. Around the corner, over the tracks, down an alley, through the transit authority carriage depot and up a creaky flight of stairs, they came to a rough door, on which were stenciled the words, "The Space, LLC." Inside, the Fox introduced Pinocchio to Deward X. Cassel-Dworkin, who was the founder and artistic director there. The man was dressed in second-hand androgynous clothing, Birkenstocks, and a dirty watchpersun's cap, so his artistic credentials were obviously beyond reproach.

"I'm so very *excited* to meet you, M. Pinocchio," the artistic director purred. "Mmmmm, I can tell already you'd fit in *perfectly* with our 'family' here. *Speaking* of family, do you have any wealthy uncles or aunts who would be interested in *underwriting* the efforts of creative explorers such as *we?*"

Pinocchio had to say no, sadly, that he could only contribute the coins his craftspersun father had given him to buy books and a hot lunch. Cassel-Dworkin assured him art didn't take its inspiration from money, of course, and enrolled him in the training center right away. For the privilege of such tutelage, the puppet handed over all his cash. (The Fox and the Cat also took a fairly hefty agent's cut.) And with that, Pinocchio rejected Geppetto's conformist agenda and moved into The Space, LLC.

At first the workshops went well. Pinocchio could feel himself growing as a performer. He enjoyed the primal scream exercises, exploring the pain of separation from his original log. He also loved hanging out with his fellow actors, nursing diner cups of coffee, getting piercings, and observing life.

The persuns of The Space, LLC, did a lot of street theater to bring more of their art to the people and save money on space rental. Times were not always lean: public and private grants came in often enough to let the troupe mount some important stagings, including a severely Brechtian interpretation of "Bye Bye Birdie."

But in time Pinocchio's star trajectory and dramatic ardor began to wane. Despite Cassel-Dworkin's promises about "alternative, nontraditional casting," Pinocchio repeatedly found himself playing coat racks and endtables. He was promised a lead role in "The Cherry Orchard," but when he learned of the violence the role required, the fledgling wooden thespian balked.

"How can I give birth to true expression in this dual-visaged environment?" he thought. "Compromise and tokenism in every direction. I won't hang around to see what they'll use me for in 'The Master Builder.'"

So, on a Monday, when everyone else was out auditioning for sitcoms and industrial shows, Pinocchio snuck out of The Space, LLC., and continued his journey in search of his true essence. He took his headshot postcards with him, though, just in case.

CHAPTER 3

*In which our hero learns the value of not
misrepresenting himself counterfactually with
a hypothetical assertion of disaccuracy.*

P inocchio had pulled back the veneer and exposed the rot of the self-indulgent theater world and its boojie, privileged attitudes. Now, the questions remained: Where would he go? What should he do? Where could a failed, unskilled actor earn a living (except politics, of course)? All the uncertainty left a knot in his stomach.

As he pondered his future, the persun of log ambled down the road winding through the forest. Traveling this way helped him calm his mind and recenter himself. The arboreal ecosystem was varied, healthy and sustainable. A few of the trees even looked familiar, though he couldn't place the phloem.

A sharp pain in his side made Pinocchio cry out. He reached over and found a wriggly biting insect trying to burrow inside him. He held the hitchhiker up for a closer look.

The bug wriggled his legs and said cheerfully, "Always insist on locally grown food!"

Pinocchio shook him roughly. "Well, why did it have to be me?"

The bug let out a little chuckle and said, "A philosopher once said, 'Tend to your own garden.' Wise words, dontcha think? Heh."

A frustrated Pinocchio got ready to turn this tiny parasite into paste, when a blinding flash of light left him visually non-functioning. The blue individual skilled in eldritch arts appeared and exclaimed, "Pinocchio! What are you doing?"

"This cricket is chewing his way inside me!"

"No no no," she corrected, "that's *not* a cricket!"

"It's not? Boy, it sure looks like . . ."

"No, it most certainly is *not,* and remind me later to instruct you about copyrighted characters and overly litigious entertainment conglomerates."

The bug piped up, "The man who represents himself in court has a fool for a client!"

"And these annoying adages! It doesn't stop! Is this what they mean by a 'microaggression'?"

The sorcerex replied, "I have invited this adorable insect along to be your conscience. He's a safeguard for your future. I'm very concerned about your puppetal growth and improvement."

Pinocchio did not like this new development one bit. Why did she think he needed a conscience? Most other persuns got along fine without one.

The bug said, "We only have one life in which to live our best, but one life should be enough," and jumped onto Pinocchio and started boring into his trunk again.

"Ow!" said the puppet. "Stop it! You're being an invasive species!"

With that, an amazing thing happened: the nose on Pinocchio's face doubled in length! Pinocchio gasped in surprise.

"And now comes Safeguard #2," the blue mystickal wommon said. "Whenever you lash back with comments that are hateful or exclusionary, your poor little nose will grow."

The puppet fumed, "That's a no-good . . ."

"Wait, I'm not finished. Your nose will also grow if you:

- Quote an unreliable news source;
- Use information you know to be untruthful, misleading or only quoted in part;
- Use abusive, profane or discriminatory language;
- Appropriate a culture not your own in a sketch, song, performance or other work, artistic or academic;
- Create a hostile work or play environment through language, deed, or signage:
- Obstruct, harass or intimidate any agent of mystickal improvement in the course of his/her/its sanctioned activities."

"Who's to say what's true or not, anyway?" he asked, and his nose immediately grew again.

"And especially if you say ignorant things like that."

"And for that, you make my nose grow?" Pinocchio sniffed, touching his new wooden protuberance gingerly. "Pretty lookist punishment, don't you think?"

"My hands are tied. The sensitivity classes have been full for a year."

"What did I say that was so wrong?"

"Your comment about the bug was unkind, defamatory and speciesist. It didn't take his own situation into account. He might have arrived here because of climate change, in which case he'd be a displaced, climate-refugee bug. He's a worthwhile species who just happens to be invasive."

"Wait! You said you brought him here! How the —"

She fluttered in an off-putting manner. "If you have a complaint, you can register it following the procedures outlined in the pamphlet."

"What? What pamphlet?"

"The pamphlet being mailed to you, which you should receive in seven to ten business days."

"A moment of silence in a moment of anger," the bug chuckled from inside Pinocchio, "will save 100 moments of regret. Ha ha!"

"Aaargh!" the puppet yelled. "Why did you have to make my conscience so corny? He's a living, breathing, *biting* Hallmark card." And with that comment, his nose grew again.

"You'd better keep your judgments in check," the sayer of sooth said, "unless you'd like a nose that needs training wheels."

Pinocchio thought this over for a minute. He didn't want to be saddled with a conscience that would merely pile on guilt and reinforce a moral system unsuited to the needs of a modern world. But the sooner he did as the naggy sensitivity trainer asked, the sooner she would leave him alone.

"If anyone was offended by my statements," he said, in a classic dodge, "I offer an apology." And the blue wommon, not well versed in public relations or double-speak, took Pinocchio at his word. Immediately, a flock of birds flew onto his nasal extremity, and pecked and pecked until it was its original size again, thus providing a solution that appeased all parties in a completely organic (though not unpainful) way.

"There," said the persun of enhanced aethereality, "all back to how it was. Your conscience will help guide you, dear Pinocchio. Do not resist it. I cannot be with you all the time. Behave yourself, embrace the truth, and you will be rewarded."

Pinocchio smiled and nodded, but didn't say anything. Though her endorsement of the status quo sent shivers down his rings, he decided it was best to feign agreement. Soon she said farewell in another flash of light, and the optically assaulted Pinocchio was again left with the decision of where to go and how to get rid of the bug while making it look like an accident.

CHAPTER 4

In which our hero tries to
find some order in anarchy.

Pinocchio and his chitinous conscience (still unnamed, for reasons explained in the previous chapter, and definitely not wearing a little top hat, morning coat or spats) continued down the road through the forest. The insect still spouted little bromides with the zeal of great epiphanies.

"Every end is a new beginning!"

"Worry is the down-payment on a problem you may never have! Ha ha!"

"Sometimes 'home' is another person!"

The bug's clichés were starting to grate on Pinocchio even worse than its rasping mandibles. The puppetic individual grew more determined than ever to get rid of the bug, regardless of the ecological impact.

Like many a literary hero/shero/theyro, Pinocchio was determined to discover his destiny on his own. Geppetto and the fairy and the insect were useless to him, he thought, even though one had carved him, one had given him life, and one was teaching him a simplistic, hidebound system of right and wrong gathered from plaques in gift shops. He had absorbed, even at this young age, the toxic masculine ideas of individual accomplishment and emotional isolation. If he ever did become a real boy, there was most certainly a heart attack in his future.

As he turned a bend in the road, Pinocchio was surprised to hear the murmur of a crowd. Very soon, he began to see people, a few to start, then more and more. The excitement of the throng began to build, and in time they all amassed on an open grassy plain, chanting, shouting, and raising fists. As Pinocchio walked through the mob, he heard and saw a myriad of new ideas he found very exciting.

A firm hand to the chest stopped Pinocchio in his tracks. "Heeeeeey, where d'ya t'ink *yer* goin'?" asked a young man with a comically archaic accent once attributable to the white ethnic, economically marginalized population quintile of New York City, chewing on a blade of grass.

"Who, me?"

"Yeah, youse," was the reply, "wit' da stars in his eyes. Ain't ya never been to a rally before? Who are ya, anyway?"

"I'm Pinocchio," he said. "Who are you?"

"For copyright and a few udder reasons, who I yam ain't important. Ain't important, I tell ya! You look like da kinda boid who wants t' make his mark on da woild, am I right?"

"Uh-huh," he nodded, "that's right!"

"Den you've come to da right place, my li'l puppet pal. Dis is the biggest protest rally yer ever gonna see! Look around youse, and see all the groups fightin' fer change. And fightin' wit' demselves, too, heh heh, like always."

"Change for what?"

"Whadda I look like, a genius?" he asked. "Who knows? My advice: smash it all an' worry about it later. See ya 'round, sucker." And off walked the red-headed instigator, happy to "troll" those who were working for positive social change.

(With apologies to any actual trolls, ogres or gnomes who might happen to be reading this.)

So Pinocchio roamed among the groups, one after another, and learned what they had to offer. He followed a group carrying a black flag (which of course made the bug nervous). "We're anarchists," they told him. "We want to smash all oppressive social structures, and then wait for persunkind's natural goodness to emerge from the ashes. The best system is NO system! Come to our meeting later."

"Gosh," Pinocchio said. "Where will you be holding your meeting?"

"We haven't agreed on that yet — haven't for 35 years — and we're *proud* of it!"

The woke puppet found himself among marchers of all kinds: some who wanted to tear down the patriarchy, some who wanted to resurrect a matriarchy, some who felt technology was the salvation of the future, some who thought technology was the enemy of the future, some who felt they *themselves* were the enemy of the future. With each new group he came upon, their slogans resonated so much with him that he readily agreed to march alongside them. He found everyone fascinating (except for the insensitive lout who invited him to attend the Burning Man festival). The bug, who was growing very seasick with all this back-and-forth, wheezed, "Never make someone a priority when all you are to them is an option. *Urp.*"

At the edge of the clearing was a ravine, with a rushing river down a few hundred feet below. Pinocchio noticed on the opposite side groups that were waving their own flags and signs, and yelling very nasty things to the people on his side.

"Who are they?" he asked no one in particular.

"Evil! Stupid! Hateful! Burn them! Destroy them!" came his answer, from both sides of the chasm. And that was answer enough for everybody.

Eventually, Pinocchio learned about all sorts of new things: bandanna masks, flash mobs, pepper spray, and Molotov cocktails (ouch!). And when he got bored with the message of one group — like all cis-gendered males, he had a very short attention span — there was always another group nearby with another appealing message to follow.

In one such group that was trying to save the planet by wiping out hamburger consumption (named W.I.M.P.Y — "World Is Meat-Poisoned, Yo!"), he met a young wommon named Kasha. She was a wyld wommon, beautiful and free, and the growth she inspired in the persun of wood was obvious. He admired her knowledge and passion. He also wanted someone who could help guide him through this chaotic world without blinding him with a blue flash every time she showed up.

So after a W.I.M.P.Y. meeting, in which they planned to blow up a few franchise locations of a globe-strangling fast-food chain, Pinocchio screwed down his courage and said, "If I may say so, Kasha, I like you."

"You have my permission," Kasha said. "I like you too, Pinocchio. You really understand so much. You have an old soul."

"Oh, I wouldn't say that," he said, embarrassed by the feeling of his young sap rising.

"Don't put the key to your happiness in someone else's pocket," opined the bug, though it was burrowed too deeply in to be heard.

"You're very rooted," Kasha smiled, "and stand tall in your beliefs."

Pinocchio said loudly, "No doubt in my mind, hamburgers are the thing that's going to destroy the earth!"

While his statement wasn't surprising, the reaction was, as his nose doubled in length!

"Aggh!" Kasha exclaimed. "What's going on?"

Pinocchio stammered, "It-it's an allergic reaction to the pepper spray."

And with that alternative fact, his nose doubled in length again.

"What are you doing? You pig!"

"Let me tell you a story, so you can understand. There was this blue fairy, see . . ."

"Don't you *dare* puppet-splain to me! I know sexual harassment when I see it! I've been assaulted! I've been violated!"

And with that Kasha picked up a large stick and began to chase Pinocchio. Others who saw his growing proboscis were shocked and shouted at him as well. As he ran to escape, many startled people in the crowd were lucky his protruding nose didn't spear them.

Pinocchio ran from the angry Kasha so hard and so fast that he didn't see where he was going and ran headlong over the edge of the ravine. He tumbled over and over in the air, then splashed in the river and was swept away. While Kasha went to seek counseling about the incident, others on her side of the ravine erected a safety fence along the edge. Those on the far side, meanwhile, hooted and jeered and set off guns and fireworks, occasionally falling over the edge themselves, rejoicing in their liberty to do so.

CHAPTER 5

In which Pinocchio gets
waterlogged in the cradle of life.

The river carried Pinocchio mile after mile, reminding any persuns watching from shore of the perils of deforestation. In the cold water, his nose, like so many things do, shrank to a tiny size. Soon the current picked up speed, propelling him through several river ecosystems and out to the open sea. Though weathered and worn, Pinocchio looked forward to this new adventure. He'd often dreamed of seeing the ocean and believed he'd always had a little nautical sap in him. (His grandmother, it can be truthfully told, had been carved years earlier into an empowering bi-species mermaid for the prow of a ship.)

The bug stuck out his head and smiled, "You can't stop the waves, but you can learn to surf!" At which point, to Pinocchio's relief, a hungry salmon swam up and ate it.

This unexpected respite gave Pinocchio a chance to ruminate on his life so far. The seagulls whirling overhead and the whisperings of the waves helped him confront his feelings unvarnished. He thought of Geppetto, the individual who happened to be a fairy, the deceptive Fox and Cat, Deward

X. Cassel-Dworkin, the unforgettable Kasha. He had some affection for them all, but they also tried to make him conform to those ancient rigid norms of what a live puppet should be, those unfair assumptions about stringless marionettes that society never seems to discard. Just because he was optimistic and carefree didn't deny him the right to *not* be those things, to explore the whole wide panoply of mannequinism, to break out of the little wooden box people wanted to put him in, to splinter the stifling puppet paradigm . . .

His self-indulgent reverie was interrupted by a large whale, as it breached the surface with a mighty splash. In an instant, it caught Pinocchio in its mouth and dragged him into the brine-fortified deep!

Now, let's stop for some clarification before our narrow cultural biases get the better of us.

For centuries, whales have had the undeserved reputation for gobbling persuns (and now puppets) whole, and maliciously to boot. We can "thank" the Judeo-Christian tradition for the vertically gifted tale of Jonah being ingested this way, not to mention the Leviathan, which the Old Testament says "God" created to frighten persunkind into staying meek and subservient. We can also acknowledge the American Romantic school of literature for projecting all its fears and inadequacies in the face of uncaring Nature onto the innocent figure of Moby-Dick.

So, rather than perpetuate the misconceptions about these gentle giants of the deep — the largest creatures on earth known to sing! — we'll be specific and scientifically accurate in this story and state that Pinocchio did *not* get fully swallowed by the whale, but merely became lodged in its baleen. And who should be stuck next to him in the baleen but his father, temporally accomplished Geppetto!

"Father! What are you doing here?"

Geppetto's head lolled slowly around. His watery frolic

with the magnificent sea creature was providing negative benefits. "What . . . who's there?"

"It's me, Father, Pinocchio!"

"What . . . sorry," he tried to speak as he spat out sea water, "the name's not familiar . . ."

"Not familiar? I left for school just three days ago."

"Well, you know . . . busy life . . ."

The whale submerged at that point and stayed under for quite some time. When it emerged again, both man and mannequin gasped for air.

"I'd heard krill . . . was a new superfood," Geppetto choked, "but you can have it . . ."

Pinocchio turned and said, "*Now* do you recognize me?"

Geppetto sighed and said, "Oh, who cares what an old man thinks anyway?"

"Enough with the passive-aggressiveness! Own your emotions!"

Just at that moment, the magickal azure individual appeared and floated in the air next to the two detainees. She had a disappointed look in her eyes when she saw these wet, miserable creatures.

"Is this how you have your fun now, joy-riding in the mouth of an innocent whale?" she asked. "You think Nature is just here for your amusement? I'm really very disappointed in you, Pinocchio."

Pinocchio would have defended himself, had the whale not submerged again in a hunt for food.

"And you, Geppetto," she continued, "a fine example for a father figure to make. What will you be teaching him next? Grenade fishing?"

Geppetto could not defend himself either, for he had long ago passed out from exhaustion and now almost completely drowned.

"Stop all your shaming!" Pinocchio said, coughing seawater. "It's already enough that you swoop in to solve things like a know-it-all. You don't have to hammer it home!"

"Do you think I like being your *dea ex machina?*" she asked, pointing her wand in his face rather aggressively. "This isn't my area of expertise."

"Why are you bothering us, then?"

"I told you before, it's a side gig. I'm also an adjunct professor of medieval studies and folklore, but that doesn't pay diddly and I'm up to my wingtips in student debt. Magic's a job that pays okay, but I want tenure."

"Elitist," the puppet muttered, unheard.

"Now, since I have an extension class to teach tonight, let's get this over with. Let me talk to the whale; I'm sure it's as annoyed by this whole situation as I am."

So the persun of nymphal experience flew over to the side of the whale's head and clicked and squeaked a few syllables into its ear hole. In an instant, the cetaceous individual turned and headed for the undeveloped shoreline far in the distance.

CHAPTER 6

In which our peripatetic
puppet fulfills his destiny.

O n an isolated beach, the right (though not more deserving) whale did the right (for our story) thing. Avoiding the nesting migration of a herd of sea turtles and mindful of not grounding itself, the whale swam to a safe distance from the shore and blew the puppet and the puppet-maker onto the beach like a couple of cherry pits. They sputtered and coughed, thanked the whale for its generosity, and plopped down on the sand exhausted.

"I'll admit, it's good to see you, Pinocchio," Geppetto finally said. "I didn't know what to do with myself after you disappeared. Just a lonely co-dependent old man . . ."

"I've missed you too, Father, despite your penchant for guilt trips."

". . . just the persun who carved you and brought you into this world, is all."

Again, a blue flash exploded in front of them. "Yet I was the one," said the individual who happened to be a fairy, "who gave him life."

"But who was the absentee parent, flying away all the time?" Geppetto countered.

"Dad! Mom! Stop fighting!"

The magickal plot-mover smiled. "You are right, wise Pinocchio. This should be a happy reunion. The family is back together!"

Geppetto let out a long sigh. "Yes, well, this 'family' thing is a losing proposition for me, I've found. Too much investment, not enough return. I'm not made for it."

Pinocchio's chin dropped on its hinge. "What do you mean?" he gulped emotionally.

"I mean, in today's world, we pay so much lip service to the concept of a 'happy family' that it's inevitable we all become dissatisfied. No one can live up to the ideal. Besides, I'm not ready to be a father."

"Not ready? You're 75!" the puppetic individual said.

"But I *am* ready to monetize this. There are lots of people too lonely or too busy to pay attention to their actual family. But I could carve them one, to their exact specifications! Big, small, all conforming to conventional beauty standards — now they can be surrounded by the family they want, whenever they want. Already happening in Japan, I hear. So, goodbye, I wish you luck! You've had your chance to roam for fame and fortune. Now it's my turn."

Geppetto got up and walked out of sight down the beach, just another man abdicating his responsibilities. Pinocchio felt like crying.

"How disappointing," the sorcerex sighed. "If only he were made of wood . . ."

Pinocchio said, "Who'd have thought so much commercial exploitation was in my background? Brings up the whole Nature vs. Nurture question, doesn't it? Lucky for me my natural parents weren't hummon."

"Pinocchio," she said, "I'm not your birth mother, or your birth tree, but I'm very proud of you nonetheless. You have taken your quest for persunal evolution seriously, if somewhat erratically. Your inclusive heart and your social conscience both grew, along with your nose."

"It's the journey, not the destination, that matters," he mused, wincing at the idea that the bug's stale adages had had an effect on him.

"Bravo, well spoken. And now, because of your honesty and hard work, I will reward you by turning you into a real, live . . ."

"If you're going to say 'boy,' then stop right there. I told you in the beginning not to assume that I wanted to become a hummon, especially not a male. One thing I've learned in my travels is that I don't want to join a group that's so destructive and hateful to the planet and other species, as well as to themselves."

The individual with wizardly skills was stunned and embarrassed for a moment. "Yes, you're right, you did tell me that. Well, I'm sort of at a loss then. Most animate and inanimate beings I meet in my line of work want to become hummon — and usually rich, handsome and happy for the rest of their lives."

"Oh, how shallow," Pinocchio scoffed. "I really pity such creatures, clamoring to be something they're not. My adventures have taught me to accept myself, knots and all. In my quest for meaning, I've found so much of my nurturing, fertile side that I know exactly what I would like to become!"

"And what is that, my dearest Pinocchio?"

Pinocchio thrust out his chest and said proudly, "A pile of mulch!"

And so concludes our story of the little ligneous homunculus. The persun of fairyhood granted Pinocchio's wish and transformed him into a rich, fertile mulch that she later spread around the rose bushes in her garden. Now, whenever there is a bloom, it greets her with a tiny "Hello" and she thinks of her formerly wooden friend.

As for Geppetto, his grand dreams of a puppet companion empire failed to materialize, mostly due to stiff competition from the sexbot industry. He returned to his small village and carved more figures from found and repurposed wood. To stay busy (and to prepare for the possible appearance of another Pinocchio), he often performed puppet shows in the village square for the local pre-adults. Among his shows, the most popular was an update of a classic deemed too violent for a modern audience, which he reinvented as "Listen Supportively and Judy."

And the individual who happened to be a fairy, inspired by Pinocchio's youthful enthusiasm, gave up her efforts for academic tenure. Instead, she assembled a devoted following of volunteers — dolls, mannequins, crash-test dummies and effigies of all kinds — animated both by magick and by progressive ideals. She ran for office and won in a landslide. In a short time, she helped pass consumer fraud legislation (to deal with the Fox and the Cat), environmental protection statutes (for the whale and the bug) and the abolition of the Electoral College (because, *come on!*) She ushered in an era of prosperity and fairness, and everyone lived happily ever after, whatever state their carbon happened to be.

About the Author

James Finn Garner is best known as the author of *Politically Correct Bedtime Stories,* which was a #1 New York Times best-seller, and its two sequels, *Once Upon a More Enlightened Time* and *Politically Correct Holiday Stories,* both of which were also NYT best-sellers. The first book of this trilogy has been translated into more than 20 languages, and they have all been enjoyed in countries around the world, including China, Turkey, Indonesia and Iran. His other books include *Tea Party Fairy Tales, Apocalypse WOW!* and *Recut Madness: Favorite Movies Retold for Your Partisan Pleasure.*

His latest work is the clown noir mystery series starring "Rex Koko, Private Clown": *Honk Honk, My Darling; Double Indignity; The Wet Nose of Danger;* and the upcoming *Notoriousness.* These hard-boiled, big-shoed thrillers are available in print and electronic editions. In addition, *Honk Honk, My Darling* is available as a dramatic podcast. Check out RexKoko.com for the inside dope and a face full of fizz water.

He is the custodian of Bardball.com, a website that aims to resurrect the art of baseball doggerel. Bardball is a fan-driven site that publishes new poetry every weekday during the regular season, and welcomes reader submissions, both lofty and lascivious.

Finally, for those who like pictures with their words, there's Garner's webcomic, created with this book's designer, Airan Wright. Single White Vigilante follows the exploits of a superhero in the throes of midlife, including speed-dating, calcifying musical knowledge, and drunk-dialing his arch-enemies in prison. A Justice-Regret Cocktail, with Swords, it can be found at www.singlewhitevigilante.com.

Made in the USA
Las Vegas, NV
11 March 2021

19392223R00024